Where Your Treasure Lies

30 Day Devotional

Ryan Youngre

Copyright 2025
Globe Shakers Publishing Co.
www.globeshakers.com

This book or any parts thereof may not be reproduced in any form, or transmitted by any means; electronic, mechanical, photocopy, recording or otherwise is not permitted without prior written permission of the author.

All rights reserved
Printed in the United States of America

Bulk orders dangerousloveryan@gmail.com

Table of Contents

Day 1	Prioritizing What Matters Most
Day 2	Trusting God for the Desires of Heart
Day 3	Seek 1st HIS Kingdom
Day 4	The Choice Between 2 Masters
Day 5	Commit Your Plans to the Lord
Day 6	What Will it Profit You?
Day 7	Fleeing Youthful Passions
Day 8	Working as for the Lord
Day 9	Trusting God's Provision
Day 10	God's Faithful Supply
Day 11	The Foolish Wealthy Man
Day 12	Priorities in the Temple of God
Day 13	Fixing Our Hope on God
Day 14	Treasures in Heaven
Day 15	Transforming Your Mind
Day 16	The Value of the Soul
Day 17	Faithfulness in the Small Things
Day 18	God as the Source of Our Provision
Day 19	The Blessing of Trusting in the Lord
Day 20	The Blessing of Obedience
Day 21	Rooted in His Word
Day 22	Living in Christ
Day 23	Returning to Our 1st Love
Day 24	Overflowing with Hope
Day 25	The Overflow of Blessings
Day 26	The Blessing of Giving
Day 27	The Illusion of Wealth
Day 28	The Righteous and the Wicked
Day 29	Contentment in God's Presence
Day 30	The Danger of Loving Money

Day 1: Prioritizing What Matters Most

"For where your treasure is, there your heart will be also." — Matthew 6:21 (NIV)

We live in a world full of distractions, where so many things compete for our attention and affection. From careers, to relationships, to material possessions, to social media, it's easy for our hearts to become divided, chasing after fleeting things. But in Matthew 6:21, Jesus points us to a profound truth: *"Where your treasure is, there your heart will be also."*

The word "treasure" in this verse doesn't just refer to money or material wealth—it includes anything we hold dear, invest in, or prioritize. It could be our time, our ambitions, our relationships, or even our comfort and security. Jesus is urging us to examine where we place our trust and energy, because whatever we treasure most will inevitably claim our hearts.

Where you invest your time and energy, your heart follows: Our hearts are naturally drawn to what we value most. If we spend the majority of our time chasing success or possessions, our hearts will become centered around those pursuits. But if we invest in our relationship with God, our hearts will grow closer to Him.

True treasure is found in God: Jesus invites us to treasure things of eternal value—like love, kindness, peace, and righteousness. When we treasure God's Word, His presence, and His purpose, we are investing in treasures that will never fade or disappoint.

The call to prioritize: We must intentionally choose to place God at the center of our lives. This requires taking a step back and evaluating what matters most to us. Are we prioritizing God's Kingdom and His will over temporary, earthly things?

Take some time today to reflect on your life and evaluate where your treasure lies. What are the things you are spending your time, resources, and energy on? Are they things that align with God's will for your life, or are they distractions? Ask God to help you realign your priorities, that your heart may follow after His will and His Kingdom.

Prayer: Dear God, thank You for Your Word and the wisdom it offers. Help me to examine my heart today. Reveal to me the things that may not align with Your will for my life. I want to treasure You above all else. Guide me in putting You first, so that my heart will be fully devoted to You. In Jesus' name, Amen.

Day 2: Trusting God for the Desires of Your Heart

"Take delight in the LORD, and he will give you the desires of your heart." —Psalm 37:4 (NIV)

Many people dream of achieving a better lifestyle, believing that hard work alone is the key to success. While diligence is important, this perspective can oversimplify the journey and overlook significant challenges. Systemic barriers, lack of opportunities, and intentional sabotage can often stand in the way, no matter how much effort is applied.

This reality can be disheartening, but as believers, we are reminded that our hope and provision come from the Lord, not solely from our efforts or circumstances. Psalm 37:4 invites us to take delight in the Lord, trusting Him to fulfill the desires of our hearts.

To "delight in the Lord" means to find joy and satisfaction in His presence, aligning our desires with His will. It is through this intimate relationship with Him that our perspectives shift, and we gain strength to face life's challenges.

When we delight in God, our Desires Align with His Purpose. As we grow closer to Him, our hearts

Where Your Treasure Lies

begin to long for the things He desires for us—things that glorify Him and bring true fulfillment.

While obstacles may seem insurmountable, God has the power to open doors that no one can shut. He equips us to navigate systemic challenges and opposition with grace and perseverance.

Even when life feels unfair, His presence provides peace and assurance. We can trust that He sees our struggles and works all things together for our good (Romans 8:28). By focusing on God and His promises, we can find peace in knowing that He holds our future. True fulfillment comes not from striving alone, but from trusting the One who gives us the desires of our hearts.

Real success is shaped by more than just effort. It requires acknowledging the role of external factors while maintaining faith in God's ability to work through and beyond them. This balance allows us to: 1) Remain humble, recognizing that every blessing comes from Him. 2) Show compassion for others who face struggles we may not fully understand. 3) Persist with resilience, knowing that God is faithful to His promises.

Prayer: Heavenly Father, Thank You for the reminder that true success begins with delighting in You. Help me to align my desires with Your will and to trust You, even when challenges arise. Teach me to rely on Your strength and guidance as I pursue the purpose You have for my life. Grant me compassion for others who face difficulties and remind me that Your grace is sufficient for every need. In Jesus' name, Amen.

Day 3: Seek First His Kingdom

"But seek first the kingdom of God and his righteousness, and all these things will be given to you as well." —Matthew 6:33 (NIV)

In this powerful verse from Matthew, Jesus gives us a profound promise that can radically transform our lives. He calls us to prioritize God's Kingdom above everything else. When we focus on seeking God and living in His righteousness, He assures us that all the things we need — both materially and spiritually — will be provided.

The world often tells us to chase success, wealth, and security as the ultimate goals of life. It pressures us to constantly strive for more and more, convincing us that happiness and fulfillment are found in what we acquire or achieve. But Jesus flips this mindset on its head. He invites us to seek something far greater — the Kingdom of God.

When we seek God's Kingdom, we are pursuing His will, His presence, and His purpose for our lives. Seeking His righteousness means aligning our hearts and actions with His values, living in a way that reflects His character. This pursuit isn't about perfection, but about a genuine desire to live according to God's standards, trusting that He will guide us.

Where Your Treasure Lies

The promise here is not just that we will receive material provision, but that when we focus on God's Kingdom first, everything else falls into place. He knows what we need and will ensure that we are taken care of. The pressure to worry about the future, the "what-ifs," and the fear of not having enough can be released when we trust in God's faithful provision.

Trust God's Provision: Sometimes, the weight of our struggles comes from worrying about the unknown — finances, relationships, or career. Jesus calls us to trust that when we put him first, He will provide all our needs. Shift your focus away from what you lack and place your trust in the One who provides abundantly.

Closing Thought: When we seek God first, everything else finds its proper place. The anxiety of "having it all" fades as we trust that God, who knows what we need, will supply all things. Let us pursue His Kingdom with the confidence that He is our ultimate provider.

Prayer: Lord, thank You for the promise that when I seek Your Kingdom and Your righteousness first, You will take care of all my needs. Help me to trust You fully and to make You my first priority every day. Remove the hindrances and worries that pull me away from You. I surrender my desires, my goals, and my future into Your hands, knowing You are faithful to provide. In Jesus' name, Amen.

Day 4: The Choice Between Two Masters

"No one can serve two masters. Either you will hate the one and love the other, or you will be devoted to the one and despise the other. You cannot serve both God and money." —Matthew 6:24 (NIV)

In this powerful verse from Matthew, Jesus reveals a profound truth about the nature of our hearts: we can only be truly devoted to one master. In the context of this passage, Jesus highlights two masters — God and money — and declares that they are incompatible.

The challenge here is not just about wealth or financial success, but about the foundations and values that shape our lives. Money, while necessary for survival, is not meant to be our master. It is a tool for serving God's kingdom and providing for our needs, but it should never become the driving force of our lives.

Jesus understands the human tendency to hold onto things that give us security, status, or comfort. Yet, He warns that when we give our hearts to money, we risk allowing it to dominate our thoughts, decisions, and ultimately our worship. We cannot give our full loyalty to God while simultaneously allowing the pursuit of wealth or material possessions to consume us.

Where Your Treasure Lies

The Choice: Jesus calls us to choose. We must ask ourselves: 1) Who or what holds the highest place in my heart? 2) Do I make decisions based on what will bring me closer to God or what will bring me more material gain? 3) Am I willing to sacrifice my comforts for the sake of God's kingdom?

If we're honest, many of us struggle with the pull of money and material success. The world encourages us to pursue wealth, possessions, and status, but Jesus reminds us that true fulfillment comes only from serving God, not from accumulating things. God is the only one worthy of our complete devotion.

Consider how you can use your wealth and resources to serve others, contribute to God's work, and further His Kingdom on earth.

Closing Thought: When we choose to serve God wholeheartedly, we gain a peace and fulfillment that money can never provide. Choose wisely, for in God's service, there is eternal joy and purpose beyond the fleeting rewards of this world.

Prayer: Lord, thank You for reminding me that I cannot serve both You and money. Help me to recognize the areas in my life where I have allowed material pursuits to become too important. Teach me to trust You fully and to place You first in all things. May my heart be devoted to Your purposes, and may I use the resources You have blessed me with to further Your Kingdom. In Jesus' name, Amen.

Day 5: Commit Your Plans to the Lord

"Commit to the LORD whatever you do, and he will establish your plans." —Proverbs 16:3 (NIV)

In life, we are often driven by goals, ambitions, and plans. Whether it's in our careers, relationships, or personal growth, we seek direction and hope for success. Proverbs 16:3 reminds us of a powerful truth: when we commit our actions and plans to the Lord, He will establish them.

To "commit" means to entrust or dedicate something to God. It's not about simply asking for His blessing on our existing plans but surrendering them to His will. This verse encourages us to actively seek God's guidance in everything we do, acknowledging that He is the one who directs our steps. By submitting our plans to Him, we place our trust in His wisdom and timing, knowing that His ways are higher than ours.

When we commit our work, decisions, and desires to the Lord, He aligns them with His perfect purposes. This does not mean that everything will go as we expect, but it does mean that we can trust God's sovereignty and provision in every situation. His involvement in our plans brings stability and purpose, even when the path seems unclear.

Where Your Treasure Lies

Surrender Your Plans to God: Before making any decision or pursuing any goal, take time to commit it to God in prayer. Ask for His guidance and wisdom, and trust that He will direct your steps. Be open to His leading, even if it leads in a different direction than you anticipated.

Trust in His Timing: God's timing is always perfect, even when it doesn't match our expectations. Trust that when you commit your plans to Him, He will establish them in His time. If things don't unfold as you expect, remember that God is still at work and has your best interest in mind.

Closing Thought: When we commit our work to the Lord, we can be confident that He will establish our plans. The peace that comes from knowing God is in control helps us navigate life with faith, trusting that His purposes will always prevail. Let Him lead you today in all you do.

Prayer: Lord, I commit all my plans and desires to You. I surrender my ambitions, my goals, and my future into Your hands. Guide me, Lord, and establish my plans according to Your will. I trust that You know what is best for me, and I seek to align my heart with Yours. Help me to be patient and trusting in Your perfect timing. In Jesus' name, Amen.

Day 6: What Will it Profit You?

"What good is it for someone to gain the whole world, yet forfeit their soul? Or what can anyone give in exchange for their soul?"
—Mark 8:36-37 (NIV)

In these verses, Jesus challenges us to consider the true cost of pursuing worldly success at the expense of our spiritual well-being. He asks us, "What good is it to gain the whole world, yet forfeit your soul?" In other words, no matter how much wealth, fame, or power we accumulate, it means nothing if it comes at the cost of our relationship with God and our eternal destiny.

In the pursuit of success, it can be easy to lose sight of what truly matters. Society often measures success by material wealth, status, or achievements. But Jesus reminds us that all the riches and accomplishments in the world are temporary. They are ultimately empty if they are disconnected from God's purpose for our lives. When we make the pursuit of earthly things our highest priority, we risk losing what is most important: our soul.

The question Jesus poses is not just about wealth or possessions; it's about the choices we make every day. What are we willing to sacrifice for the sake of gaining the things of this world? Are we willing to

Where Your Treasure Lies

trade our integrity, our peace, or our relationship with God for temporary success? The reality is that nothing in this world can compare to the eternal value of a soul surrendered to God.

Application: Take a moment to reflect on where your heart is focused. Are you chasing after things that will pass away, or are you seeking God's Kingdom and righteousness above all else? Ask yourself if your daily choices reflect a commitment to eternal values or fleeting ambitions.

Guard Your Soul: Jesus calls us to protect our souls from the temptations of the world. The pursuit of success, while not inherently wrong, can become dangerous if it leads us away from God. Make intentional decisions to invest in your spiritual growth, your relationship with God, and your eternal well-being.

Live with Eternity in Mind: Keep the big picture in view. Everything in this life is temporary, but your soul will last forever. Ask yourself, "How am I living today to honor God and prepare for eternity?" Choose to pursue eternal goals over temporary gains, knowing that what you gain in Christ is far more valuable than anything this world has to offer.

Closing Thought: No amount of wealth, fame, or success can compare to the value of your soul in God's eyes. The pursuit of earthly things is temporary, but when we choose to live for God, we invest in what is eternal. Let us live each day in a way that reflects the eternal worth of our soul, trusting that in Christ, we gain what is truly priceless.

Prayer: Lord, help me to recognize the fleeting nature of worldly success. Guide my heart to seek You above all else and to value my relationship with You more than anything the world can offer. Protect my soul from the temptations of this world and help me to live with eternity in mind. I want to honor You in all that I do and make choices that reflect Your love and purpose for my life. In Jesus' name, Amen.

Where Your Treasure Lies

Day 7: Fleeing Youthful Passions

"So flee youthful passions and pursue righteousness, faith, love, and peace, along with those who call on the Lord from a pure heart."
—2 Timothy 2:22 (ESV)

In 2 Timothy 2:22, Paul urges Timothy—and us—to flee from youthful passions, which represent temptations like pride, lust, and selfish ambition. These desires can easily lead us astray. Instead, we are called to pursue righteousness, faith, love, and peace.

Righteousness is living in line with God's will, while faith is trusting in His promises even through tough times. Love is selfless, following the example of Christ, and peace is the calm assurance that comes from knowing God and being in harmony with Him.

Paul also emphasizes the importance of walking with others who share our desire for godliness. We are not meant to walk this journey alone but should surround ourselves with those who call on God from a pure heart.

Evaluate Your Passions: Reflect on areas where youthful passions might be leading you astray. Ask

God to help you resist temptations and focus on His will.

Pursue Righteousness: Set intentional goals to live out righteousness, faith, love, and peace in your life, and do so in fellowship with other believers.

Closing Thought: Let's choose daily to flee from deterrents and walk in the virtues that bring us closer to God. Together, we can live out these principles with pure hearts, trusting in God's strength for the journey.

Prayer: Lord, thank You for Your guidance. Help us flee from temptations and live holy. Give us another measure of faith, love, and peace. Surround us with a community that encourages our growth in purity and devotion. In Jesus' name, Amen.

Where Your Treasure Lies

Day 8: Working as for the Lord

"Whatever you do, work heartily, as for the Lord and not for men." — Colossians 3:23 (ESV)

In our daily lives, work can sometimes feel like a series of tasks to check off a list. Whether it's a demanding job, household chores, or even volunteer work, we often go through the motions without thinking about the purpose behind it. However, Colossians 3:23 provides us with a powerful reminder that our work is not just for our earthly bosses, clients, or families—ultimately, it is for the Lord.

Paul, in his letter to the Colossians, is urging believers to shift their mindset about work. He is inviting us to see our daily responsibilities as acts of worship. It's easy to feel disconnected from the significance of our tasks, but when we approach work with the understanding that we are doing it for God, it transforms how we engage with each task.

Think about your work today: How can you do it *heartily*—with passion, dedication, and excellence—knowing that God is your ultimate audience? Whether you're doing something mundane or fulfilling, God sees the effort and the heart behind it. He values the faithfulness with which you serve, and He can use even the most ordinary tasks for His glory.

Work with purpose: Every task, no matter how small, can be an opportunity to serve God. Even in a challenging job, remember that you're part of something greater. This mindset helps transform frustration into fulfillment, knowing that your efforts are part of God's greater plan.

Give your best: Working "heartily" means putting your best effort into everything you do. It's not about perfection, but about striving for excellence in the work God has entrusted to you. When we give our best, we honor God and become a reflection of His character.

Closing Thought: No matter what you do, do it as an offering to the Lord. When we work for Him, our tasks become acts of worship, and our labor is not in vain.

Prayer: Lord, thank You for reminding me that my work has eternal value. Help me to approach each task, big or small, with a heart that desires to honor You. May I work with excellence, integrity, and joy, knowing that my efforts are ultimately for You. Transform my perspective on work, and help me to see every task as an opportunity to serve You and glorify Your name. In Jesus' name, Amen.

Where Your Treasure Lies

Day 9: Trusting God's Provision

"Therefore I tell you, do not be anxious about your life, what you will eat, nor about your body, what you will wear. For life is more than food, and the body more than clothing. Consider the ravens: they neither sow nor reap, they have neither storehouse nor barn, and yet God feeds them. Of how much more value are you than the birds!"
— Luke 12:22-24 (ESV)

In today's fast-paced world, anxiety about the future is something many of us face. We worry about finances, health, relationships, and the unknowns of tomorrow. Jesus, in this passage from Luke, reminds us of a simple yet profound truth: We are more valuable to God than the birds of the air, and He promises to provide for us.

Consider the ravens. They don't plant crops or store food in barns, yet God, in His infinite care, provides for them. These birds don't worry about where their next meal will come from, and yet they are always fed. How much more will God, who loves us deeply, provide for us?

Jesus is calling us to trust in God's provision. Anxiety often arises from a fear that God won't meet our needs, or from the desire to control every aspect of our lives. But Jesus teaches us that worry is unproductive; it does not add a single hour to our life. Instead of worrying, we are called to focus on seeking God's kingdom, trusting that when we prioritize Him, He will take care of the rest.

Release control: Identify areas where you're holding on tightly out of fear. Surrender those areas to God, trusting that He will provide. Let go of the need to control every outcome and allow God to lead.

Practice gratitude: Reflect on how God has already provided for you. Make a list of His faithfulness—both the big and small things—and use it as a reminder to trust Him more deeply in times of uncertainty.

Closing Thought: When anxiety creeps in, remind yourself that God, who feeds the birds of the air, will surely take care of you. Trust Him, and seek His kingdom first, for in doing so, you will experience the peace that surpasses all understanding.

Prayer: Father, thank You for Your faithfulness. Help me to trust You more deeply, especially when anxiety tries to take hold of my heart. Just as You care for the ravens, I know You will care for me. Teach me to release my worries and seek Your kingdom above all else. May I rest in the knowledge that You are good, and You will always meet my needs. In Jesus' name, Amen.

Where Your Treasure Lies

Day 10: God's Faithful Supply

"And my God shall supply all your need according to His riches in glory by Christ Jesus."
—Philippians 4:19 (NKJV)

As humans, we often find ourselves worrying even about the simplest matters. We might think that our worth is tied to how much we have or how well we're doing. But as we grow in our walk with the Lord, we begin to understand that our true source of provision comes from God alone.

In Philippians 4:19, Paul reminds us that our Heavenly Father knows exactly what we need and promises to supply it, not based on our own efforts or abilities, but according to His riches in glory. This isn't just about material needs—it's about emotional, spiritual, and relational provision. When we align our plans with God's will and seek His kingdom first (as Jesus said in Matthew 6:33), we can trust that He will take care of everything else.

It's easy to let fear or insecurity creep in when we feel like we don't have control over our circumstances. We may begin to focus on what we lack or what we think we need. But the truth is, God has already provided all that we need in Christ. When we prioritize His kingdom and trust in His provision, we release the burden of trying to do it all ourselves. God doesn't just provide for us in a limited way; He does so abundantly, out of His glorious riches.

Align Your Priorities: Are you prioritizing things that distract you from seeking God's kingdom first? Take time to assess your life and simplify where necessary to make space for what truly matters.

Release Your Worries: Whatever you are stressing about—finances, relationships, or career—take a moment to surrender those concerns to God. He is faithful to meet all your needs.

Closing Thought: When we seek God first, we can experience peace, knowing that our needs are met by the Creator of the universe. Misplaced priorities and fears melt away when we remember that God's riches are limitless, and He will provide everything we need according to His perfect will.

Prayer: Lord, I confess that at times I have allowed worry and fear to overshadow my trust in Your ability to meet my needs. I am reminded today that You know my situation, and I can rely on Your faithfulness. Help me to seek Your kingdom first and trust that You will provide for me in every area of my life. Teach me to live with an open hand, knowing that You supply all my needs according to Your glorious riches in Christ Jesus. Thank You for Your abundant care. In Jesus' name, Amen.

Where Your Treasure Lies

Day 11: The Foolish Wealthy Man

"Then someone called from the crowd, 'Teacher, tell my brother to divide the inheritance with me.'
Jesus replied, 'Man, who appointed me a judge or an arbiter between you?'
Then he said to them, 'Watch out! Be on your guard against all kinds of greed; life does not consist in an abundance of possessions.'
And he told them this parable: 'The ground of a certain rich man yielded an abundant harvest. He thought to himself, "What shall I do? I have no place to store my crops."
Then he said, "This is what I'll do. I will tear down my barns and build bigger ones, and there I will store my surplus grain.
And I'll say to myself, 'You have plenty of grain laid up for many years. Take life easy; eat, drink, and be merry.'"
But God said to him, "You fool! This very night your life will be demanded from you. Then who will get what you have prepared for yourself?"
This is how it will be with whoever stores up things for themselves but is not rich toward God.'"
—Luke 12:13-21 (NIV)

In this parable, Jesus presents a striking contrast between earthly wealth and spiritual richness. The rich man in the story is consumed by his success.

His crops have yielded more than enough, so he decides to store them up, build bigger barns, and focus on self-indulgence. His plans are all about preserving his wealth and enjoying comfort for the rest of his life. He says to himself, "Take life easy; eat, drink, and be merry," forgetting that life is more than wealth and ease.

However, God's response is sobering: "You fool! This very night your life will be demanded from you." The man's focus on earthly accumulation left him unprepared for the most important thing—the condition of his soul.

The man's problem wasn't that he was wealthy, but that his devotions were misplaced. He trusted in his possessions to bring him security and joy, but he neglected the eternal treasure of being rich toward God. Jesus warns us about all kinds of greed—those desires to accumulate more for ourselves, often at the cost of others or at the expense of what truly matters.

Guard Your Heart Against Greed: Like the rich man, we can easily become fixated on accumulating wealth or securing our future through material things. But Jesus cautions us to watch out for greed. Ask yourself: Where are you placing your security and trust? Is it in your possessions, your career, or in God's resources?

Focus on What's Eternal: Wealth can decline, but God's kingdom is eternal. Rather than storing up treasures on earth, Jesus calls us to invest in what truly matters: relationships, service, love, and faith. Being "rich toward God" means valuing His kingdom and seeking His righteousness above all else.

Live with an Eternal Perspective: The rich man thought he had many years to enjoy his wealth, but he was not prepared for eternity. Life is uncertain, and we are called to live with the awareness that we are stewards of all we have. What are we doing with the time, talents, and treasures God has entrusted to us?

Prayer: Heavenly Father, help us to remember that life is more than possessions. Open our eyes to see that our true wealth is found in our relationship with You. Teach us to be rich toward You, focusing not on earthly gains but on eternal rewards. Guard our hearts against greed and help us to trust in Your provision. May we live each day with an eternal perspective, seeking Your kingdom first. In Jesus' name, Amen.

Day 12: Priorities and the Temple of God

"Is it a time for you yourselves to be living in your paneled houses, while this house remains a ruin?"
—Haggai 1:4 (NIV)

In the book of Haggai, we encounter a convicting question from God: "Is it time for you yourselves to dwell in your paneled houses, while this temple lies in ruins?" This question is directed at the people of Israel after they had returned from exile and began rebuilding their lives, but neglected the rebuilding of God's house—the temple.

The Israelites had focused on securing their own comfort and personal prosperity. They invested time, energy, and resources into their homes, making them "paneled"—a sign of luxury and self-indulgence. Meanwhile, the temple, which symbolized God's presence and His glory, lay in ruins. God was calling them to reassess their priorities. They were content to focus on their own homes, while the house of God, the very place that represented His greatness and the heart of their worship, was left desolate.

This isn't just a historical moment; it's a reflection of the human tendency to prioritize personal comfort over spiritual devotion. When we become preoccupied with our own desires—our homes, careers, entertainment, and pleasures—it's easy to let our relationship with God fall by the wayside. We may not consciously choose to neglect God, but our actions can reveal where our true priorities lie.

Build God's House First: For the Israelites, the temple was a representation of God's presence among them. Today, we are the temple of the Holy Spirit (1 Corinthians 6:19), and God desires to dwell within us. Are we nurturing our relationship with God? Are we spending intimate time in prayer, worship, and studying His Word? Building God's house means making space for His presence in our daily lives.

Respond to God's Call: When God spoke through Haggai, He didn't just point out the neglect of the temple; He called the people to action. Similarly, God is calling us to make changes where necessary—to realign our priorities and take action to put Him first in every area of our lives.

Prayer: Heavenly Father, forgive us for the times we have focused more on our own comfort than on Your glory. We confess that we often allow the things of this world to distract us from what truly matters. Help us to place You at the center of our lives. May we be faithful stewards of the time, talents, and resources You've given us, always remembering that we are called to honor You first. Fill our hearts with a desire to build Your house, to nurture our relationship with You, and to reflect Your glory in all we do. In Jesus' name, Amen.

Day 13: Fixing Our Hope on God

"Instruct those who are rich in this present world not to be arrogant nor to put their hope in wealth, which is so uncertain, but to put their hope in God, who richly provides us with everything for our enjoyment." —1 Timothy 6:18 (NIV)

In 1 Timothy 6:18, the apostle Paul offers a vital piece of advice to those who are wealthy in the world's eyes: not to place their trust in the unstable nature of riches but to fix their hope on God, the true provider. The pursuit of finances, while not inherently wrong, can easily lead us to trust in material things more than in God's faithfulness. The riches of this world are uncertain—they can be lost, stolen, or devalued at any moment. In a world that promises security through wealth, Paul reminds us that the only true and lasting security comes from God alone.

Riches can make us feel self-sufficient and independent, but they can also bring arrogance, worry, and a false sense of control. When our hope is in wealth, we are left vulnerable to anxiety, because wealth is never guaranteed. However, when we place our trust in God, we can be sure of His provision and care for us. God has richly provided us with everything we need—not just to survive, but to enjoy life. He is the ultimate source of security, joy, and satisfaction.

Guard Against the Temptation of Wealth: Paul is not condemning wealth, but he is warning against the temptation to place our hope in it. If you are financially well-off, consider whether your trust is more in your bank account than in God. If you are struggling financially, remember that your worth and security are not determined by how much money you have. True security comes from trusting in God, not in material possessions. He is faithful to provide for your needs, and He has already given you the greatest gift—His Son, Jesus Christ. In every season, make a conscious decision to fix your hope on Him.

Live Generously: Paul instructs the wealthy not only to avoid putting their trust in money, but also to be rich in good deeds and generosity. Those who have been blessed with wealth are called to use it for God's kingdom—to share with others and to help those in need. When we focus on being a blessing to others, we shift our perspective from the uncertainty of wealth to the eternal value of generosity.

Prayer: Heavenly Father, thank You for being the source of all that we need. Forgive us for the times when we've placed our trust in wealth and possessions instead of in You. Help us to remember that joy come from You alone. We ask that You guide us in managing the resources You've given us, and that we may use them to bless others and advance Your kingdom. In Jesus' name, Amen.

Day 14: Treasures in Heaven

"Do not store up for yourselves treasures on earth, where moths and vermin destroy, and where thieves break in and steal. But store up for yourselves treasures in heaven, where moths and vermin do not destroy, and where thieves do not break in and steal." —
Matthew 6:19-20 (NIV)

In this passage from the Sermon on the Mount, Jesus invites us to reflect on where we are placing our trust and affection. He contrasts two kinds of treasures: earthly treasures, which are temporary and vulnerable, and heavenly treasures, which are eternal and secure. Earthly treasures—such as wealth, possessions, and achievements—can fade away. They can be destroyed, lost, or stolen. Yet, we often find ourselves investing much of our time and energy in accumulating these things, believing they will bring us lasting satisfaction and security.

Jesus, however, points us to a different kind of treasure. He encourages us to "store up treasures in heaven," where nothing can corrupt, decay, or be taken away. These heavenly treasures are found in our relationship with God, in acts of love and service to others, in obedience to His will, and in the eternal rewards that come from living a life devoted to Him. When we shift our focus on advancing His kingdom, our hearts are aligned with what truly matters—things that have eternal significance.

Where Your Treasure Lies

The key principle Jesus teaches here is that where our treasure is, there our hearts will also be. If our focus is on accumulating wealth and possessions, our hearts will be set on earthly things. If our focus is on serving God and storing up heavenly treasures, our hearts will be aligned with God's values. What we treasure reflects what we truly value and love. Where is your heart? What does it reveal about your heart posture?

Pursue Heavenly Treasures: Jesus invites us to store up treasures in heaven, which can be done by living in obedience to God, loving others, sharing the gospel, and using our resources for His kingdom. Consider how you can shift your focus from temporary gains to eternal investments. Perhaps there are areas of your life where God is calling you to be more generous, compassionate, or faithful.

Align Your Heart with God's Kingdom: The treasure of heaven isn't just something we can accumulate—it's about aligning our hearts with God's will. When we pursue God's purposes and live according to His Word, we are building a life that reflects His love and priorities. Ask God to help you desire the things He desires and to keep your heart focused on what truly lasts.

Prayer: Heavenly Father, thank You for the eternal treasures You offer us through a relationship with You. Forgive us for the times we have placed our hope and trust in the things of this world. Help us to store up treasures in heaven, where our hearts can be secure in You. Teach us to value what You value—loving others, living faithfully, and serving Your kingdom. May our hearts be fully aligned with Your will, and may our lives reflect the treasure of knowing You. In Jesus' name, Amen.

Day 15: Transforming Your Mind

"Do not conform to the pattern of this world, but be transformed by the renewing of your mind. Then you will be able to test and approve what God's will is—His good, pleasing, and perfect will."
—Romans 12:2 (NIV)

In this powerful verse, the apostle Paul urges us not to conform to the patterns and values of this world. The world around us constantly pressures us to follow its ways: to idolize materialism, success, status, and comfort. The culture around us promotes values that often conflict with God's kingdom—selfishness over selflessness, appearance over character, instant gratification over long-term purpose. If we're not careful, we can easily begin to mirror these worldly ideals, allowing them to shape how we think, act, and live.

However, Paul offers us a better way—transformation. Rather than being conformed to the world, we are called to be transformed by the renewing of our minds. This transformation begins in the heart and the mind, as we allow God's Word and His Spirit to reshape our thoughts, desires, and actions. Transformation is not something we can achieve on our own; it's a work that God does in us when we open ourselves to His influence and guidance.

The renewal of the mind is a daily process. It requires spending time in prayer, studying Scripture, and meditating on God's truth. As our minds are renewed, we begin to see the world differently—from God's perspective. We start to understand what is truly valuable, what pleases God, and what leads to a life of fulfillment. The result is that we can "test and approve" what God's will is for us—living in a way that is good, pleasing, and perfect in His sight.

Be Mindful of the World's Influence: The world has a subtle way of shaping our thoughts and behaviors, often without us even realizing it. Take a moment to reflect on how the world's values may be influencing you—whether through media, culture, relationships, or even your own ambitions. Ask God to reveal areas where you may be conforming to worldly patterns and to help you realign your thoughts with His truth. Engage with God's truth not as a mere routine but as a way to realign your heart and mind with His will. Meditate on God's promises and let His Word challenge and inspire you to live in a way that reflects His character.

Test and Approve God's Will: As your mind is renewed, you will begin to discern God's will for your life more clearly. Transformation enables you to understand what is truly important and to make decisions that align with His purpose for you. Trust that God's will is good, pleasing, and perfect, and seek to live in a way that honors Him in every aspect of your life.

Prayer: Heavenly Father, thank You for calling us to a life of transformation. We acknowledge that the world often tries to shape our thoughts and desires in ways that are not in line with Your will. We ask for Your help to renew our minds daily, so that we can discern Your will and live according to Your purposes. Transform our hearts and minds, that we may honor You and reflect Your goodness. Guide us as we seek to follow You and live out the calling You've placed on our lives. In Jesus' name, Amen.

Where Your Treasure Lies

Day 16: The Value of the Soul

"What good will it be for someone to gain the whole world, yet forfeit their soul? Or what can anyone give in exchange for their soul?"
—Matthew 16:26 (NIV)

In the fast-paced, goal-driven world we live in, it's easy to get caught up in the pursuit of success, wealth, and recognition. We often set our sights on achieving more — a higher salary, a bigger house, a more impressive career — believing that these accomplishments will bring lasting happiness and fulfillment. But in the quiet moments, when we pause to reflect, we can't help but wonder: What is it all for? When we pursue the things of this world at the expense of our souls, we lose what is most precious — our connection to the Creator. Let us remember that no achievement or possession is worth more than the eternal life and peace that come from living for God.

Jesus' words challenge us to evaluate what we are truly living for and to recognize the ultimate value of our souls. Our souls are eternal. They are the core of who we are, shaped by God's love and created for a relationship with Him. The pursuit of earthly things, though they may bring temporary satisfaction, cannot fill the void or secure the peace that only God can offer. In fact, Jesus warns that the things we chase after — when placed above our spiritual well-being — can lead to the forfeiture of our soul's true purpose.

Reflect on Your Priorities: Take a moment to consider what you're investing your time, energy, and heart into. Are you striving for success and recognition at the cost of your relationship with God or your inner peace? It's easy to let the busyness of life overshadow the true calling to follow Jesus.

Seek Eternal Values: Remember that our souls are meant to find satisfaction in the eternal, not the temporal. Invest in your relationship with God. Spend time in prayer, worship, and Scripture. True fulfillment comes when we align our priorities with God's will.

Choose What Lasts: The things of this world may seem valuable, but they don't last. Choose what has eternal significance — love, kindness, integrity, and faith. These are the treasures that will enrich your soul and carry you through this life into eternity.

Prayer: Lord, thank You for reminding me of the true value of my soul. Help me to see the temporary nature of the things I often chase after and to focus on what lasts forever — my relationship with You. Guide me to live a life that honors You, where my actions reflect Your love and truth. I trust that You are enough, and that nothing in this world can compare to the eternal joy of knowing You. Amen.

Where Your Treasure Lies

Day 17: Faithfulness in the Small Things

"Whoever can be trusted with very little can also be trusted with much, and whoever is dishonest with very little will also be dishonest with much. So if you have not been trustworthy in handling worldly wealth, who will trust you with true riches?"
—Luke 16:10-11 (NIV)

In our world, it's easy to measure success by the big things — a promotion, a new car, a house, or even a position of influence. We often imagine that when we finally reach a place of power or wealth, we will be able to make a greater impact. But Jesus flips this thinking on its head by emphasizing that faithfulness starts with the "little things."

In Luke 16:10-11, Jesus teaches us a powerful principle: If we are trustworthy in the small tasks — whether that's managing finances, being honest in our relationships, or using our time wisely — we prove ourselves capable of handling much more. On the other hand, if we are dishonest or neglectful in the small things, it will eventually show in the bigger areas of life.

We are entrusted with "worldly wealth" — money, possessions, time — not as an end in itself but as a test. Jesus is challenging us to consider how we manage what has been given to us. Are we faithful with the resources we have? Are we generous? Are we wise stewards? In the same way, God entrusts us with "true riches" — His love, His word, His Kingdom work — when we prove faithful with the small things in our lives.

Jesus values honesty and integrity, even in the smallest of matters. When we are faithful in these, it builds trust in us and prepares us for greater opportunities. Ask God for the strength to be trustworthy in the little things, knowing that faithfulness in the small tasks will open the door for greater things. Recognize that everything you have — your money, time, abilities, relationships — is a gift from God. How you manage these resources reflects your relationship with Him. Be diligent in using them for His glory and the benefit of others. Stewardship is not just about managing resources, but about showing God that He can trust you with more.

Closing Thought: Our faithfulness in the small things opens the door to greater opportunities and responsibilities.

Prayer: Lord, thank You for the resources and responsibilities You've entrusted to me. Help me to be faithful in the small things, knowing that they are not insignificant to You. Give me wisdom to manage my time, finances, and relationships in a way that honors You. I desire to be trustworthy in all things, so that You may trust me with the greater responsibilities You have for my life. Teach me to live with integrity and to steward all that You've given me for Your Kingdom. Amen.

Where Your Treasure Lies

Day 18: God as the Source of Our Provision

"But remember the LORD your God, for it is he who gives you the ability to produce wealth, and so confirms his covenant, which he swore to your ancestors, as it is today."
—Deuteronomy 8:18 (NIV)

In a world where success is often credited to hard work, intelligence, or luck, it's easy to forget the true source of our provision. We may look at our accomplishments and think we are the ones responsible for our success, but Deuteronomy 8:18 reminds us that it is the LORD who gives us the ability to produce wealth. Every skill, talent, opportunity, and resource we have comes from God.

God's covenant with His people is one of care and provision. He is not just a distant Creator but a loving Father who desires to bless His children. This verse is not only a reminder of God's ongoing covenant with us but also an invitation to acknowledge Him as the ultimate source of everything we have. It's easy to become self-reliant, thinking we control our prosperity, but God calls us to remember that all we have comes from Him.

When we acknowledge God's provision, we are called to steward what He has given us wisely, generously, and with gratitude. Wealth is not just for personal comfort but for the advancement of

God's Kingdom. The ability to work, to create, to produce, and to give is a gift from God that confirms His faithfulness. In the same way God provided for the Israelites in the wilderness, He provides for us today, and we are to honor Him by using what He has given us for His glory.

When you experience success, remember to thank Him for His hand in your life. This helps keep our hearts humble and centered on God rather than self. Gratitude is a natural response when we realize that God is the one who gives us the ability to produce wealth. Cultivate an attitude of thankfulness for everything you have, and use your blessings to serve others and bring glory to God.

Prayer: Lord, thank You for being the source of all that I have. Thank You for giving me the ability to work and produce, and for providing for my every need. Help me to remember that all I have comes from You, and to live with a heart of gratitude and stewardship. Teach me to use my resources wisely and generously for Your purposes, and help me honor You in everything I do. May my wealth and success reflect Your goodness and faithfulness. Amen.

Where Your Treasure Lies

Day 19: The Blessing of Trusting in the Lord

"But blessed is the one who trusts in the LORD, whose confidence is in him."
—Jeremiah 17:7 (NIV)

In a world full of uncertainty and shifting circumstances, it's easy to place our confidence in the things that seem stable — our jobs, our bank accounts, our relationships, or even our own abilities. But these things, as good as they may be, are ultimately not the foundation we were meant to rely on. Jeremiah 17:7 directs us to the only sure source of blessing: **trusting in the LORD.**

This verse reminds us that true blessing comes not from what we possess or achieve but from having unwavering confidence in God. To trust in the Lord means to place our hope, reliance, and security in Him alone. It's an active choice, a declaration that no matter what happens in life — whether in times of plenty or want, peace or trouble — we trust God's faithfulness and goodness.

When we place our trust in God, we find stability, peace, and strength. The world around us may change, but God's promises remain secure. Trusting in God brings blessings because it positions us to receive His guidance, His provision, and His peace. It shifts our focus from our own efforts to His unchanging character, and it gives us the confidence that He is with us in every season of life.

Rest in God's Blessing: Trusting in God brings peace and rest, knowing that He is in control. Whatever difficulties you face, remind yourself of God's sovereignty and His promise to never leave or forsake you. Allow your confidence in Him to lead you to a place of peace that surpasses understanding.

Closing Thought: When we choose to trust in the Lord, we open the door to true blessing. No matter what circumstances we face, placing our confidence in God leads to peace, strength, and the assurance that He is with us. Let us trust in Him today and experience the blessing that comes from relying on His unfailing love.

Prayer: Lord, thank You for being a trustworthy God. I confess that I often place my confidence in things that are temporary and uncertain. Help me to place my full trust in You. Strengthen my faith and remind me of Your unshakable promises. Teach me to rely on You in every area of my life, knowing that You are always faithful. I choose to trust in You, Lord, and I believe that You will bless me as I place my confidence in Your goodness. Amen.

Where Your Treasure Lies

Day 20: The Blessing of Obedience

"And observe what the LORD your God requires: Walk in obedience to him, and keep his decrees and commands, his laws and regulations, as written in the Law of Moses. Do this so that you may prosper in all you do and wherever you go."
—1 Kings 2:3 (NIV)

In 1 Kings 2:3, King David gives his son Solomon a powerful and timeless piece of advice: **obedience to God brings prosperity**. This wasn't just a general instruction but a reminder of God's covenant promises — that when His people walk in obedience, they experience His blessing and guidance in all aspects of their lives.

Obedience is not just about following a set of rules; it is about choosing to align our hearts and actions with God's will. It's an act of trust, acknowledging that His commands are for our good and that He knows what is best for us. When we follow God's ways, we open the door to His favor, wisdom, and direction. This obedience leads to prosperity — not just in material wealth, but in our relationships, peace of mind, and spiritual growth.

God's laws are not meant to limit us, but to guide us to a life of flourishing. David's instruction to Solomon serves as a reminder that true success comes when we prioritize God's Word and walk in His ways. Obedience to God sets us on a path where we can experience His abundant life, no matter where we go. Invite God to reveal areas where you can grow in obedience, and trust that He will guide you.

Obedience is not a one-time decision, but a daily practice. In every decision you make, choose to walk in obedience to God's will, whether in your work, relationships, or personal choices. Trust that as you do, God will bless and guide you in all you do.

Closing Thought: When we walk in obedience to God, we open the door to His favor and blessing. Prosperity is not just about wealth but about living a life that reflects God's goodness and brings Him glory. Let us choose obedience as the path to true success, trusting that God will prosper us in all that we do.

Prayer: Lord, thank You for Your commandments that guide me toward a life of blessing and prosperity. Help me to walk in obedience to Your Word, knowing that it is for my good. Give me the strength to align my will with Yours and to trust in Your wisdom. I desire to prosper in all that I do and go, not just in earthly success, but in spiritual growth, peace, and purpose. Help me to live in obedience to You every day. Amen.

Where Your Treasure Lies

Day 21: Rooted in His Word

"Blessed is the one who does not walk in step with the wicked or stand in the way that sinners take or sit in the company of mockers, but whose delight is in the law of the LORD, and who meditates on his law day and night. That person is like a tree planted by streams of water, which yields its fruit in season and whose leaf does not wither—whatever they do prospers."
— Psalm 1:1-3

The message is clear: aligning ourselves with the values of the world will lead us to spiritual dryness, while delighting in God's Word will lead to abundant life. This challenges us to examine our associations. The "wicked," "sinners," and "mockers" represent those who reject God's truth, and their ways lead to destruction. To walk in their ways, stand with them, or sit with them means to align ourselves with their attitudes, behaviors, and values. Conversely, the psalmist calls us to avoid such paths. But this isn't just about avoiding the wrong—it's about pursuing the RIGHT.

The key to a flourishing life is delighting in the law of the LORD. God's Word is not a burden but a delight for those who understand its beauty, wisdom, and transformative power. It's not just about knowing the scriptures but about meditating on them, letting them shape our thoughts, actions, and desires. When we let God's Word sink deep into our hearts, it reshapes our character and directs our lives.

This image of a tree planted by streams of water is one of stability and vitality. The tree doesn't rely on seasonal rains or external circumstances. It draws life continually from the water source, ensuring it remains fruitful and thriving regardless of external conditions. Similarly, when we root ourselves in God's Word, we remain spiritually nourished, producing fruit in season. Our "leaves" do not wither; our faith remains strong, our hearts full, and our lives impactful.

God promises that those who are firmly rooted in His Word will prosper in whatever they do. This doesn't necessarily mean material wealth or worldly success but a life that flourishes in peace, joy, purpose, and eternal significance. Our prosperity lies in the flourishing of our souls, our relationships, and our service to others. When we study God's Word, our lives mirror His character, and that alignment brings about His blessing.

Take time today to examine your associations, your conversations, and your inner circle. Choose to surround yourself with those who point you toward God.

Closing Thought: When we root ourselves in God's Word, we find that no matter the storms or seasons, we remain grounded, fruitful, and full of life. Keep your roots deep, and you will surely see the fruit of God's blessing in your life.

Where Your Treasure Lies

Prayer: Heavenly Father, I thank You for the gift of Your Word. I desire to be like the tree planted by streams of water, thriving in Your truth and bearing fruit in season. Help me to delight in Your Word and meditate on it day and night. Guard me from the influences of the wicked and sinners and lead me to those who will encourage me in Your ways. May my life reflect the prosperity that comes from walking with You. In Jesus' name, Amen.

Day 22: Living in Christ

"I have been crucified with Christ and I no longer live, but Christ lives in me. The life I now live in the body, I live by faith in the Son of God, who loved me and gave himself for me."
— *Galatians 2:20*

In this powerful verse from Galatians, Paul declares that he has been "crucified with Christ," meaning that his old self, with all its sinful desires and self-centered ambitions, has been put to death. But this is not the end—it is the beginning of a new life, one where Christ Himself takes residence in us.

To be crucified with Christ means to fully identify with His death. When we place our faith in Jesus, we symbolically share in His death and burial. Our old life, along with its destructive patterns, is no longer our identity. We are no longer defined by our past mistakes, failures, or shame. The most profound reality for every believer is that it is no longer we who live, but Christ who lives in us. We are no longer living in our own strength; we are living in His strength. His resurrection life is now at work within us, enabling us to walk in a manner worthy of Him.

Paul goes on to say that the life he now lives in the body is "by faith in the Son of God." Living by faith means that we trust not in our own abilities, not in our own understanding, but in Jesus Christ. It's a daily surrender to His leadership and a reliance on His power. This faith is not merely intellectual assent but is a deep, abiding trust in the one who loves us and gave Himself for us. Our actions, attitudes, and choices flow out of this faith in the Son of God. Our lives are no longer ours to control but are submitted to Him.

The foundation of this new life is the incredible love of Jesus. Paul writes that Christ "loved me and gave himself for me." This love is not distant or abstract—it is personal. He gave Himself on the cross not because we were worthy, but because He chose to love us. This love is what motivates us to live for Him. It is a love that changes everything.

Closing Thought: The life we now live is not a life of striving or self-sufficiency. It is a life of complete dependence on Jesus, the one who loved us and gave Himself for us. As we walk in this reality, we experience the true freedom and purpose that come from being crucified with Christ and living by His grace.

Prayer: Lord Jesus, thank You for loving me so deeply that You gave Yourself for me. Thank You for the gift of new life through Your death and resurrection. Help me to live each day by faith in You, trusting that it is no longer I who live, but Christ who lives in me. Strengthen my heart and mind to fully embrace this new identity, and may my life reflect Your love and power. In Your name, Amen.

Day 23: Returning to Our First Love

"Yet I hold this against you: You have forsaken the love you had at first."
— Revelation 2:4

In this verse, Jesus speaks to the church in Ephesus, a church commended for their hard work, perseverance, and commitment to truth. They were known for their efforts to combat false teachings, and their unwavering stance for righteousness. Yet, despite all their commendable actions, Jesus tells them that He holds one thing against them—they have forsaken the love they had at first. Their faith had become more about duty and obligation rather than the overflow of a heart full of love for Christ. This verse serves as a powerful reminder for us to reflect on our own relationship with Christ. Are we still in awe of His love for us, or have we drifted from that passionate, intimate love we once had?

To "forsake" means to abandon or neglect. The church in Ephesus didn't lose their love for Christ—they abandoned it. Over time, other things crept in that took the place of their passionate devotion to Him. For us, it can happen in similar ways. We can become distracted by the busyness of life, the pursuit of success, or the demands of daily responsibilities. Our love for Jesus can become more about routines and obligations than about

Where Your Treasure Lies

enjoying His presence and experiencing the depth of His love.

The love we have for Jesus is not just the starting point of our faith; it is meant to be the sustaining force throughout our entire walk with Him. Jesus desires a relationship with us—one that is vibrant, passionate, and rooted in love. It is in this love that we find our true motivation for living a holy life, serving others, and fulfilling His purposes for us. When we lose sight of our first love, everything else becomes hollow and empty. Our actions, though good, become disconnected from the heart of the Gospel.

To rekindle our love for Jesus, we need to return to the basics. Spend time in prayer, not out of obligation, but out of a desire to connect with Him. Open your Bible with a heart of expectancy, remembering the joy of discovering His Word. Engage in worship, not because it's the right thing to do, but because you long to express your love for Him.

Closing Thought: Jesus is not just concerned with what we do; He is concerned with why we do it. Let your heart burn with love for Christ again, so that all you do—whether in work, worship, or service—flows from the deep well of a passionate love for Him. Return to your first love, and allow Jesus to rekindle the fire in your heart.

Prayer: Lord Jesus, forgive me for the times I have forsaken the love I once had for You. I acknowledge that life's distractions and my own priorities have caused me to lose the passion and intimacy I had with You. I remember the joy of knowing You, and I repent for allowing other things to take Your place. Help me to return to my first love, to delight in Your presence, and to live out my faith with passion and devotion. Renew my heart, Lord, and make me whole again. In Your name, Amen.

Where Your Treasure Lies

Day 24: Overflowing with Hope

"May the God of hope fill you with all joy and peace as you trust in him, so that you may overflow with hope by the power of the Holy Spirit."
—Romans 15:13

In Romans 15:13, we are reminded that hope isn't something we have to muster up on our own; it is a gift from the God of hope Himself. This verse speaks of a God who desires to fill us with joy, peace, and hope, and all we need to do is trust in Him.

But how can we experience this overflowing hope? It begins with a heart that trusts. Trusting God isn't always easy, especially when life feels out of control or when the weight of our worries seems unbearable. Yet, it's in the act of trusting Him— choosing to place our faith in His promises—that His peace and joy begin to fill our hearts. This trust creates a deep, inner transformation, where the Holy Spirit empowers us to overflow with hope, even in the midst of trials.

Trust in God: Take a moment today to surrender your worries and anxieties to God. Trust that He is with you, that He is good, and that His plans for you are filled with hope.

Ask for the Holy Spirit's Power: Pray and invite the Holy Spirit to fill you with His peace and joy. Ask that He empowers you to overflow with hope, not just for yourself but so that others may see His love and grace in your life.

Share the Hope: As you experience God's hope, share it with those around you. A kind word, an encouraging text, or a thoughtful action can bring light to someone else's darkness. Your hope, grounded in Christ, can be contagious.

Closing Thought: No matter what you're facing today, remember that you are not alone. The God of hope is with you, and through His Holy Spirit, He will empower you to overflow with hope, peace, and joy. Trust in Him, and let that hope shine brightly in your life.

Prayer: Father, thank You for being the God of hope. I ask that You fill my heart with Your joy and peace as I trust in You. I surrender my worries and fears to You, knowing that You are in control. Holy Spirit, empower me to overflow with hope, so that others may see Your love in my life. May my trust in You be a testimony of Your goodness. In Jesus' name, Amen.

Where Your Treasure Lies

Day 25: The Overflow of Blessings

"Bring the whole tithe into the storehouse, that there may be food in my house. Test me in this," says the LORD Almighty, "and see if I will not throw open the floodgates of heaven and pour out so much blessing that there will not be room enough to store it." —Malachi 3:10

In the Old Testament, the Israelites were commanded to bring their tithes—their first fruits—to God's house, the temple, as a way to honor Him and provide for the needs of the Levites, priests, and the community. In this command, God didn't just ask for obedience; He invited His people to test His faithfulness.

The idea of "testing" God may seem surprising, as we are often taught that we should never test the Lord. However, in this context, God is inviting us to trust Him with our resources, to see if He will truly fulfill His promises. He challenges us to give generously, and in return, He promises to open the floodgates of heaven and pour out blessings in abundance.

The blessings God promises are not just material but spiritual. As we honor Him with our giving, we open the door for God's provision, guidance, peace, and favor in every area of our lives. God's abundance is more than just financial—it is the peace, joy, and contentment that come when we align our hearts with His will.

Test His Faithfulness: God invites you to test Him. If you have not yet been faithful in giving, take the step to tithe and trust that God will provide. This is not about giving out of obligation but out of love and trust in God's provision.

Give with a Cheerful Heart: God loves a cheerful giver (2 Corinthians 9:7). Giving is an opportunity to experience the joy of partnership with God's work on earth. Whether in your church, community, or personal life, your generosity will bring a lasting impact.

Closing Thought: When we step out in faith to give, we are not only obeying God's command, but we are also participating in the incredible flow of blessings He has for us. Trusting God with our finances is an act of worship, and it positions us to receive His abundant grace, not just for us, but so that we can bless others.

Prayer: Lord, I thank You for Your incredible faithfulness and the promise that You will bless abundantly when I trust You with my resources. Help me to give generously and with a heart full of gratitude. May my giving be a reflection of my love for You and my trust in Your provision. In Jesus' name, Amen.

Where Your Treasure Lies

Day 26: The Blessing of Giving

"In everything I did, I showed you that by this kind of hard work we must help the weak, remembering the words the Lord Jesus himself said: 'It is more blessed to give than to receive.'" —Acts 20:35

In Acts 20:35, the apostle Paul reflects on the teachings of Jesus and demonstrates a life of sacrificial service and generosity. This powerful verse reminds us that true blessing does not come from receiving, but from giving—whether it's our time, energy, resources, or love. Jesus' words, "It is more blessed to give than to receive," flip the world's understanding of blessings on its head. In a society that often emphasizes accumulating and receiving, the kingdom of God invites us to experience the joy of selflessness and compassion.

The early church modeled this sacrificial generosity, and it's a calling that applies to us today. The blessings of giving are not just about what we offer to others but also the transformation it brings in our own hearts. As we give, we become more like Christ, who gave everything for us.

Jesus calls us to care for the weak—whether that means the physically weak, the spiritually weak, or those who are struggling emotionally or financially.

Look for opportunities to serve those who cannot repay you, remembering that in serving them, you are serving Christ.

Closing Thought: When we embrace the truth that it is more blessed to give than to receive, we shift our focus from the fleeting joys of self-centeredness to the lasting joy of serving others. In giving, we receive an even greater blessing: the opportunity to reflect Christ's heart of love. Let today be a day where you experience the true joy of selfless giving.

Prayer: Lord, thank You for the example of Jesus, who gave everything for me. Help me to live a life of generosity and service to others. Show me the weak and the needy around me, and give me the courage and resources to help them. Teach me to find joy in giving, knowing that it is more blessed to give than to receive. May my giving reflect Your love and grace in the world. In Jesus' name, Amen.

Where Your Treasure Lies

Day 27: The Illusion of Wealth

"Whoever loves money never has enough; whoever loves wealth is never satisfied with their income. This too is meaningless." —Ecclesiastes 5:10

Ecclesiastes 5:10 speaks a timeless truth that many of us have experienced or seen firsthand: the pursuit of wealth can never truly satisfy. The writer of Ecclesiastes, traditionally thought to be King Solomon, observes the vanity of chasing after money and wealth as the ultimate source of happiness and fulfillment. Even when people accumulate riches, they find that they are never enough. The hunger for more wealth continues, leading to a life of dissatisfaction and unfulfilled desire.

In today's world, it's easy to fall into the trap of equating financial success with happiness. We often believe that if we just had more money, more possessions, or more security, our problems would be solved, and we would be content. However, Solomon points out that this pursuit is ultimately "meaningless." Wealth may provide temporary comfort, but it cannot fill the deeper, soul-satisfying desires we all have.

True contentment does not come from accumulating more, but from recognizing that our ultimate worth and fulfillment are found in God, not in what we possess. When we seek God's kingdom first, we experience a peace that transcends the temporary highs and lows of financial circumstances. We begin to see that what we truly need—love, joy, purpose, and peace—is not found in material wealth, but in a relationship with our Creator.

Ask God to reveal any areas of your life where you are seeking satisfaction in material things rather than in Him.

Instead of focusing on the next financial goal or material possession, focus on investing in things that last—relationships, spiritual growth, and serving others. Seek first the Kingdom of God, and trust that He will provide for all your needs.

Prayer: Lord, thank You for reminding me that true fulfillment is not found in wealth or possessions, but in You. Help me to examine my heart and rid it of any love for money that distracts me from Your true purpose for my life. Teach me to be content with what I have, trusting in Your provision. May my satisfaction come from knowing You and living for Your glory, not chasing wealth. In Jesus' name, Amen.

Where Your Treasure Lies

Day 28: The Righteous and the Wicked

"Better the little that the righteous have than the wealth of many wicked; for the power of the wicked will be broken, but the LORD upholds the righteous."
—Psalm 37:16-17

In Psalm 37:16-17, David reminds us that even though the wicked may appear to prosper, their success is temporary. Their power will ultimately be broken, for the Lord is the true source of stability and security.

On the other hand, the righteous may not always have great material wealth, but they have something far more valuable: God's favor and protection. When we seek to live according to God's will, placing our trust in Him rather than in the pursuit of wealth or worldly success, we are assured that He will uphold us. God's righteousness is a firm foundation that will never fail, even when the things of this world pass away.

The message of this passage is not to belittle wealth or to discourage working hard for provision, but rather to shift our focus. True security comes not from accumulating wealth, but from living a life that honors God, trusting in His faithfulness to provide. The Lord blesses those who live with integrity and seek justice, and He promises to uphold them when the power of the wicked fades away.

Take some time to reflect on what you're striving for in life. Are you placing too much emphasis on material success, or are you seeking to live righteously, trusting that God will provide for you?

Choose to live righteously, even when it seems like doing so might lead to less wealth or recognition. Trust that God sees your efforts and will honor your faithfulness, even when the world may overlook you.

Closing Thought: In a world that often measures success by wealth and power, remember that the righteous are rich in the things that truly matter—God's love, peace, and protection. When we trust in Him, we discover that His provision far exceeds anything that wealth can offer, and we are secure in His hands.

Prayer: Lord, thank You for the reminder that true wealth is found in righteousness and in Your presence. Help me to trust in You and not in the fleeting promises of material success. Even if I have little, may I find my security in knowing that You uphold me and provide for my needs. Teach me to live with integrity, to seek justice, and to rest in Your faithfulness. In Jesus' name, Amen.

Where Your Treasure Lies

Day 29: Contentment in God's Presence

"Keep your lives free from the love of money and be content with what you have, because God has said, 'Never will I leave you; never will I forsake you.'"
—Hebrews 13:5

Hebrews 13:5 calls us to a life free from the love of money and to embrace contentment with what we have. In a world that constantly tells us we need more—more money, more things, more status—this command is a refreshing and counter-cultural reminder. The author of Hebrews directs our focus away from the pursuit of wealth and possessions and places it squarely on God's presence and faithfulness.

The love of money can easily lead to a cycle of dissatisfaction, where no amount is ever enough. We chase after more, thinking that it will bring fulfillment, but instead, we find ourselves caught in an endless longing. In contrast, contentment with what we have is a sign of trust in God's surplus and goodness. Contentment isn't about having everything we desire—it's about trusting that God has already given us what we truly need.

The powerful promise that accompanies this command is the assurance of God's presence: *"Never will I leave you; never will I forsake you."*

No matter what we face in life—whether times of abundance or seasons of lack—God's presence remains with us. He is our true source of peace and satisfaction. When we rest in this truth, we find that we can be content, knowing that God's love is more than enough for every need.

Assess Your Relationship with Money: Take a moment to evaluate your attitudes toward money and possessions. Are there areas where you are tempted to love money more than trusting in God? Ask God to help you detach from the pursuit of wealth and find your contentment in Him alone.

Practice Contentment: Focus on the blessings you currently have. Instead of longing for what you don't have, give thanks for what God has already provided. Contentment grows when we regularly recognize and appreciate God's goodness.

Rest in God's Promise: Whenever you feel anxious or unsatisfied, remind yourself of God's promise: He will never leave you or forsake you. You are never alone, and God's presence is enough to bring peace and security in any circumstance.

Closing Thought: In the pursuit of wealth and success, we can easily lose sight of what truly satisfies—God's presence. Contentment is not about having more, but about knowing that in Christ, we have everything we need. Trusting in God's promise to never leave us allows us to live with peace, regardless of our circumstances.

Where Your Treasure Lies

Prayer: Lord, thank You for the powerful reminder that true contentment comes from trusting in You, not in the things of this world. Help me to keep my heart free from the love of money and to be content with what You've already provided. Teach me to find peace in Your constant presence, knowing that You will never leave me or forsake me. May I always be satisfied in You. In Jesus' name, Amen.

Day 30: The Danger of Loving Money

"For the love of money is the root of all kinds of evil. Some people, eager for money, have wandered from the faith and pierced themselves with many griefs." — 1 Timothy 6:10

In 1 Timothy 6:10, the apostle Paul warns of the dangers of loving money. He doesn't say that money itself is evil; rather, it is the *love* of money that is the root of all kinds of evil. The desire for wealth, when it becomes an obsession, has the power to lead us away from God's will and into a life filled with pain, regret, and spiritual decay. It can cloud our judgment, distort our values, and even tempt us to compromise our faith.

The verse also reveals that the pursuit of money can cause deep personal grief. Those who prioritize wealth over their relationship with God may experience a restless longing that never satisfies. The more they chase after wealth, the more they lose sight of what truly matters—God's presence, peace, and purpose. This disordered desire often leads to brokenness, relational strife, and inner turmoil.

Paul's warning is not just for those who are rich, but for anyone who allows the love of money to take root in their hearts. It's easy to fall into the trap of thinking that more money will bring us happiness or security, but the truth is that only God can provide lasting peace and fulfillment. When we place our trust in Him instead of in material things, we find that our hearts are at rest.

Examine Your Heart: Take a moment to reflect on your relationship with money. Are you driven by the desire to accumulate wealth, or are you seeking contentment in what God has already provided? Ask God to help you keep money in its proper place—under His authority.

Guard Against Greed: It's easy to get caught up in the cycle of wanting more, but remember that true peace comes not from what we own, but from knowing that God is enough. Practice gratitude for what you have and focus on the eternal treasures that cannot be stolen or lost.

Seek God's Kingdom First: Jesus teaches us in Matthew 6:33 to seek first the kingdom of God, and all these things will be added to us. Make it a point to prioritize your relationship with God, knowing that He will take care of your needs. When we align our hearts with His purposes, the pursuit of wealth no longer holds power over us.

Closing Thought: The love of money promises satisfaction but delivers emptiness. Only in God can we find true fulfillment and peace. When we let go of our attachment to wealth and trust in His provision, we experience a life free from the grief that comes with chasing after things that cannot last. Let's place our hope in God alone, and allow Him to lead us to a life of true contentment.

Prayer: Lord, thank You for the reminder that the love of money can lead us away from You and cause unnecessary grief. Help me to examine my heart and remove any desire for wealth that competes with my love for You. Teach me to be content with what I have, knowing that You provide for all my needs. May I seek Your kingdom first and trust that You are more than enough for my heart. In Jesus' name, Amen.

www.ingramcontent.com/pod-product-compliance
Lightning Source LLC
Chambersburg PA
CBHW032135090426
42743CB00007B/604